A Cloudy Day

Melvin and Gilda Berger

SCHOLASTIC INC.
New York Toronto London Auckland Sydney
Mexico City New Delhi Hong Kong Buenos Aires

Photographs: Cover: Gary Crabbe/AGEfotostock;
p. 1: Mark A. Schneider/DPA (Dembinsky Photo Associates);
p. 3: Mark A. Schneider/DPA;
p. 4: Mark A. Schneider/DPA; p. 5: Mike Agliolo/Photo Researchers;
p. 6: Betts Anderson Loman/PhotoEdit; p. 7: David Young-Wolff/PhotoEdit;
p. 8: Jeff Greenberg/PhotoEdit; p. 9: Gary Crabbe/AGEfotostock;
p. 10: Anthony Bannister/Photo Researchers; p. 11: Gregory K. Scott/Photo Researchers;
p. 12: P. Michael Photoz/AKA/AGEfotostock; p. 13: Larry Mishkar/DPA;
p. 14: E.R. Degginger/DPA; p. 15: Betts Anderson Loman/PhotoEdit;
p. 16: Jeff Greenberg/PhotoEdit.

Photo Research: Sarah Longacre

ISBN 0-439-56698-3

12 11 10 9 8 7 6 5 4 5 6 7 8/0
08

Printed in the U.S.A.
First printing, October 2003

It's a cloudy day.

On a cloudy day, you
cannot see the sun.

On a cloudy day, the sun is above the clouds

On a cloudy day, you get less light from the sun.

On a cloudy day, you get less heat from the sun.

Some clouds are low.

Low clouds are made
of drops of water.

Some clouds are high.

High clouds are made of bits of ice.

Some clouds rest on the ground.

A cloud on the ground is called fog.

Some clouds bring rain.

Some clouds bring snow.

Some clouds bring storms.